This Journal Belongs To:

Printed in Great Britain
by Amazon

33788815R00059